South Huntington Public Library
145 Pidgeon Hill Road
Huntington Station, NY 11746

Famous Artists

Get to Know
Edward
Hopper

Charlotte Taylor

Enslow Publishing
101 W. 23rd Street
Suite 240
New York, NY 10011
USA
enslow.com

Published in 2016 by Enslow Publishing, LLC
101 W. 23rd Street, Suite 240, New York, NY 10011

Copyright © 2016 by Enslow Publishing, LLC
All rights reserved.

No part of this book may be reproduced by any means without the written permission of the publisher.

Library of Congress Cataloging-in-Publication Data
Taylor, Charlotte, 1978- author.
 Get to know Edward Hopper / Charlotte Taylor.
     pages cm. — (Famous artists)
 Includes bibliographical references and index.
 ISBN 978-0-7660-7222-0 (library binding)
 ISBN 978-0-7660-7220-6 (pbk)
 ISBN 978-0-7660-7221-3 (6pk)
 1. Hopper, Edward, 1882-1967—Juvenile literature. 2. Artists—United States—Biography—Juvenile literature. I. Title.
 N6537.H6T39 2016
 759.13—dc23
 [B]
                              2015026940

Printed in the United States of America

To Our Readers: We have done our best to make sure all website addresses in this book were active and appropriate when we went to press. However, the author and the publisher have no control over and assume no liability for the material available on those websites or any websites they may link to. Any comments or suggestions can be sent by e-mail to customerservice@enslow.com.

Portions of this book originally appeared in the book *Edward Hopper*: *The Life of an Artist* by Ray Spangenburg and Kit Moser.

Photo Credits: Cover, p. 1 John Loengard/The LIFE Picture Collection/Getty Images; pp. 4, 21 Photograph © 2015 Center for Creative Photography, Arizona Board of Regents/Artists Rights Society (ARS), New York. Digital image © Center for Creative Photography, The University of Arizona Foundation / Art Resource, NY; p. 7 National Portrait Gallery, Smithsonian Institution/Art Resource, NY; p. 9 © WorldPhotos/Alamy Stock Photo; p. 11 ND/Roger Viollet/Getty Images; p. 13 Album/Prisma/SuperStock; p. 15 The New York Historical Society/Archive Photos/Getty Images; p. 17 Night Shadows, 1921 (etching), Hopper, Edward (1882- 1967)/San Diego Museum of Art, USA/Museum purchase through the Edwin S. and Carol Dempster Larsen Memorial Fund/Bridgeman Images; p. 19 The 'Martha McKeen' of Wellfleet, 1944 (oil on canvas), Hopper, Edward (1882-1967)/Thyssen-Bornemisza Collection, Madrid, Spain/Photo © Boltin Picture Library/Bridgeman Images; pp. 23, 28 Art Resource, NY; p. 26 Superstock; p. 31 Smithsonian American Art Museum, Washington, DC/Art Resource, NY; p. 33 South Truro Post Office I, 1930 (w/c & pencil on paper), Hopper, Edward (1882-1967)/Private Collection/Photo © Christie's Images/ Bridgeman Images; p. 36 Edward Hopper (1882-1967). (Jo in Wyoming), (1946). Watercolor and graphite pencil on paper, Sheet: 13 15/16 x 19 15/16in. (35.4 x 50.6 cm). Whitney Museum of American Art; Josephine N. Hopper Bequest 70.1159. © Heirs of Josephine N. Hopper, licensed by the Whitney Museum of American Art. Digital image © Whitney Museum, N.Y.; p. 39 Harris & Ewing Collection/Library of Congress Prints and Photographs Division Washington, D.C.; p. 40 The House by the Railroad, 1925 (oil on canvas), Hopper, Edward (1882-1967)/Museum of Modern Art, New York, USA/Bridgeman Images; p. 41 Chop Suey, 1929 (oil on canvas), Hopper, Edward (1882-1967)/Collection of Mr. and Mrs. Barney A. Ebsworth/Bridgeman Images; p. 43 Andreas Solaro/AFP/Getty Images.

Contents

Chapter 1
Becoming an Artist 5

Chapter 2
Big Dreams 12

Chapter 3
Hopper Hits It Big 24

Chapter 4
On the Road 32

Chapter 5
A Great American Artist........ 37

Timeline............................ 44

Glossary............................ 45

Learn More 46

Index.............................. 48

Chapter 1

Becoming an Artist

Edward Hopper was a quiet man. Instead of talking, he spoke with his paintings. He was famous for painting pictures that looked real. Hopper looked for scenes that showed how he felt about life. Then, he painted them. Sometimes people asked what a painting meant. He used to say, "If you could say it in words, there'd be no reason to paint." His paintings showed Americans pictures of themselves.

Edward Hopper was born on July 22, 1882. His sister Marion was two years older. They grew up in the small town of Nyack, New York, on the Hudson River. Their mother, Elizabeth, was proud of her Dutch background. She was also proud of two ancestors who were artists. Edward's father, Garret Henry Hopper, had a dry goods (fabrics and clothing) store in Nyack. The business never did very well. So, the Hopper family lived

Get to Know Edward Hopper

with Elizabeth's mother, a widow. The house was a big, homey place on North Broadway. There was always plenty of room.

Young Artist

When Edward was seven, he got a blackboard for Christmas. It was great! He could draw anything on it. Then he could erase it all and draw a different picture. He practiced and practiced his drawing.

Edward took a pencil and paper along wherever he went. He drew everything he saw. He drew tents on camping trips and boats on the lake. He drew birds, horses, houses, people, and trains. He had a little paintbox, and he painted a sign on it. The sign said: "WOULD-BE ARTIST."

By the time Edward was twelve, he was already six feet tall! His classmates called him "Grasshopper" to tease him. He always spent a lot of time alone—reading and drawing.

His father thought Edward should spend more time outdoors. Edward used to go down to the harbor and watch the boats. The Nyack shipyards were famous for building racing yachts. Edward built his own boat when he was about fifteen. His father gave him the materials, but Edward did all the work. He later admitted that "it didn't sail very well."

Becoming an Artist

Self-Portrait (1903, National Portrait Gallery, Smithsonian Institution, Washington, DC). Hopper drew this self-portrait in 1903. It was the first year that he studied under Robert Henri.

Get to Know Edward Hopper

Studying Art

Two years later, in 1899, Edward finished high school. By now he was strong, tall, and good-looking. He had a full, wide mouth and sharp blue eyes. He had done a lot of drawing and painting. Yet, he knew he still had a lot more to learn. He decided to study drawing in nearby New York City.

Hopper entered the New York School of Art. The famous painter William Merritt Chase taught there. Every weekday, Hopper got up early and rode the train to Hoboken, New Jersey. There, he caught a ferryboat to New York.

Edward was eager to learn. He read books suggested by his teachers. He listened carefully. At school, his teachers showed him new ways to think about art. They showed him how to put feelings and ideas in his paintings and drawings. He soon became a star student in his class.

Hopper spent seven years studying art. One teacher, Robert Henri (pronounced hen-RYE), taught him a lot. Henri said that art should tell what the artist thought and felt. Henri also said to use broad brushes—not tiny ones. He told Hopper to paint large shapes and bold pictures.

Travels in Europe

More than ever, Hopper wanted to become a great artist. He knew he was still not close to his goal. He knew he needed to

Becoming an Artist

William Merritt Chase taught at the New York School of Art while Hopper was there. Chase was an American artist who became the most important art teacher of his generation.

Get to Know Edward Hopper

find his own style. To do that, he had to see more of both art and life. So, at twenty-four, he did what many other art students did in the early 1900s. He sailed for Europe.

Hopper first visited Belgium, England, Germany, and France. He visited art galleries and museums. He studied famous paintings. Finally, he arrived in Paris and stayed with a French family. Other American artists in Paris stayed up late talking, dancing, and drinking. Not Hopper. He had come to Paris to learn about painting and drawing. Hopper liked the pale, glowing light of the French capital. Later he said, "The light was different from anything I had ever known." He drew and painted everything he saw.

Hopper returned to New York in 1907. He made two more trips to Europe. In 1909, he stayed for six months, and in 1910, he visited France and Spain. After that, he never went back.

Becoming an Artist

The Louvre Museum in Paris, France, is one of the most famous art museums in the world. Hopper studied many of the paintings here.

Chapter 2

Big Dreams

Living in New York City was not cheap. Hopper needed to get a job so he could pay the rent for his studio apartment. He began doing commercial art—drawings paid for by businesses. He was good at the type of drawings used in ads and on magazine covers. He also drew pictures for stories. Hopper hated these jobs. They took precious time away from his own paintings and drawings.

In those days, few of Hopper's paintings were accepted in art shows, or exhibitions. He had been busy earning money to pay the rent and did not have time to paint new pictures good enough to show. The old ones were mostly paintings he did in France. Most Americans had never been to France. They felt these pictures had nothing to do with their lives.

Finally, in 1913, two very important things happened. Hopper found a place to live in Greenwich (pronounced

Big Dreams

Self-Portrait (1925–1930, Whitney Museum of American Art, New York). Edward Hopper painted himself as an average-looking man in a brown hat. While the artist did not do many formal self-portraits, Hopper did paint himself in his pictures.

Get to Know Edward Hopper

GREN-itch) Village. He was also asked to show his work at an important new exhibition, the 1913 Armory Show in New York.

Greenwich Village is a small neighborhood in New York. In 1913, many artists lived and worked there. Hopper moved into an apartment and studio on the top floor of a big, red brick house at 3 Washington Square North. It was a tough climb—seventy-four steps! The light up there was good for painting, though. Also, other artists lived in the building. So, even though the shy artist never spent much time with friends, he lived near other people who created art.

Hard Times

That same year, at the Armory Show, Hopper finally sold a painting! *Sailing,* a picture of a sailboat, sold for $250. It was a good price for a first sale—more than $4,300 in today's money. Perhaps he was moving in the right direction at last. Maybe he could stop drawing pictures for ads and live off the money from his own paintings. In fact, Hopper did not sell another painting for the next ten years. These were hard times for the tall, shy artist with big dreams.

So, in 1915, Hopper tried something different. He began doing etchings. Etchings are pictures, or "prints," made by carving a picture into a plate of metal or glass and using it

Big Dreams

In 1911 Hopper spent most of his time in the Greenwich Village neighborhood in New York City.

Get to Know Edward Hopper

with ink or paint to make pictures on paper. He could do several prints from one etching and sell them. Most artists used fancy swirls and complicated designs in their etchings, but not Hopper. His prints showed large, velvet-black areas of ink next to bright, white paper. Hopper's etchings seemed to capture a part of American life as it really was. They were direct and bold, and people liked them.

Hopper completed about sixty etchings between 1915 and 1923, but he made just a few prints of each one. After that, he stopped. More than anything else, he wanted to paint.

His painting did not seem to catch on, though. In 1920 Hopper had his first solo show. Sixteen of his oil paintings hung at the Whitney Studio Club. It was a great opportunity—one of the best ways for people to learn about a new artist.

Art Smarts

Oil paints are thick. The artist squeezes the paint from a tube. The paints are usually mixed to make the right shade. Often an artist will layer the paint to give the painting texture.

Big Dreams

Night Shadows (1921). Like many of his later paintings, this etching has an urban setting and realistic details.

Get to Know Edward Hopper

Every major newspaper carried the story. A reviewer called his oil paintings "truthful and sympathetic." However, he did not make any sales.

Success at Last

Hopper began to paint more oils and watercolors. By the summer of 1923, his work finally began to catch on. One of his etchings won two prizes, and reviews in the newspapers were good. He sent paintings to shows in Chicago and other cities. He also spent that summer painting watercolors in Gloucester, Massachusetts. Several other artists were there that summer. Hopper knew some of them, including Josephine Nivison. "Jo" was also a former student of Robert Henri's at the New York School of Art. The two artists spent most of that summer painting together.

Back in New York that fall, Hopper took some of his new watercolors to an art gallery. The owner told Hopper he did not like the paintings. They were "too stark," he said. By this he meant stiff, empty, and depressing. Hopper was upset. He walked out of the gallery.

Then he came to another gallery, owned by Frank Rehn. Rehn looked over the paintings. He liked them right away. He offered to take eleven of the paintings to sell. Famous collectors came to see the paintings. They liked Hopper's work.

Big Dreams

The Martha McKean of Wellfleet (1944, Thyssen-Bornemisza Museum, Madrid, Spain). Hopper was fascinated by boats and painted many of them over the years.

Get to Know Edward Hopper

Rehn sold sixteen paintings! For the rest of Hopper's life, Rehn handled all the artist's sales.

A month later, a big art exhibition in Brooklyn showed a few of Hopper's new watercolors. They were a hit! One newspaper writer exclaimed, "What vitality and force and directness!" Things were beginning to look a lot better.

Life With Jo

On July 9, 1924, Edward Hopper married Jo Nivison in New York. He was forty-two and she was forty-one. Hopper's place on Washington Square became their home and studio. Jo took the north end of the space for her workplace. Hopper took the south end. For heat, they had a big, old-fashioned pot-bellied stove. Every day, Hopper carried coal up the seventy-four stairs to their studio.

Hopper and his wife liked to live cheaply. They had no children, and they spent most of their time painting. The two painters knew they could not count on making a lot of money. So, they learned to stretch what money they had. They wore their clothes until they fell apart.

With the money they saved, they traveled. They went to Maine two summers in a row—then back to Gloucester in 1928. During their trips, they both painted.

Hopper and his wife Jo, who was also an artist, were married until Hopper's death.

Get to Know Edward Hopper

Hopper and Jo were two very different people. Jo was outgoing and said what she meant. Hopper was quiet and more polite. Jo was short and lively. Hopper was tall and awkward. They were very good friends, though, and they spent most of their time together.

Hopper continued to paint pictures of scenes along the coast. He painted lighthouses and more boats. He painted the water of the bays and inlets. He caught the way a sea breeze blows across the water. Hopper loved painting the bright summer sun. He showed the way it lit the white clapboard walls of New England houses. No one had ever before paid so much attention to these old, plain houses.

Big Dreams

The Lee Shore (1941, Private Collection). Growing up by the Hudson River influenced Hopper's early artwork. Many of his drawings showed the boats he saw all the time near his home in Nyack, New York.

Chapter 3

Hopper Hits It Big

Hopper was having some success selling his art. But in 1926, a new oil painting made a big splash. Suddenly everyone was talking about *House by the Railroad*.

Like a movie director, Hopper liked to show scenes that seemed to look in on someone's life and see a story. That is what he did when he painted *House by the Railroad*. It is a simple portrait of a house. A railroad track runs in front of it. It is a powerful, emotional painting. This grand mansion seems strange. Who lives there? Why does it stand alone and silent? Is it haunted? It is like the opening scene in a movie. It seems to begin a story. Hopper lets the viewer fill in the details.

He was forty-three years old. Hopper had waited a long time for one of his paintings to make a big hit. *House by the Railroad* was the first one that really made people talk.

Hopper Hits It Big

After that, Hopper began to paint from deep inside himself. He now knew what he wanted to "say" with his paintings. Hopper's scenes looked real. People liked the new paintings Hopper did. Some of his paintings reminded people of the countryside of their childhood. Other paintings showed city life the way it really was. For the city scenes, he used darker colors. His city scenes were sadder than his watercolors of New England. They showed that people could be lonely, even with people all around them.

Jo posed for many of Hopper's paintings. Almost every female in his paintings is Jo. Jo liked knowing she was her husband's favorite model.

Scenes From the City

Hopper showed how he felt about the city by catching it at special moments. A city is usually full of people and cars and trucks. Hopper's paintings of cities never show crowds. They show empty streets like the one in *Early Sunday Morning*. It is a picture of a business district at a time when no one is there.

"I wish I could paint more," Hopper once said. He spent lots of time sketching, especially for his oil paintings. He used yellow paper and outlined a house or scene with quick pencil lines. Sometimes, one would look especially good to him. Then he would make a painting. That did not happen often, though—only two or three times in a year! Hopper was a slow painter.

Get to Know Edward Hopper

Early Sunday Morning (1930, Whitney Museum of American Art, New York). This picture was painted at the time that the Great Depression began. Times were hard. People had very little money. The painting shows an empty street with empty stores, since Sunday is not a shopping day. There are no people around—only silence.

Hopper Hits It Big

In *Early Sunday Morning,* Hopper has stripped the scene down to its most basic parts. There are no people and we cannot read the writing on the windows. Look at the painting's lines. They are just vertical or horizontal. Hopper wanted you to feel how bare the street is.

Get to Know Edward Hopper

My Roof (1928). Hopper made the unusual choice of painting a simple roof. Some might consider this to be a dull subject. But Hopper paints the lines, shapes, and shadows in an interesting way.

Hopper Hits It Big

In Hopper's city scenes, people could recognize the kinds of places where they lived and worked. Sometimes his paintings captured silent moments. People used to stop at the corner diner on the way home from work or after a movie—the way they stop today for ice cream or coffee. Hopper caught such a scene in his most famous painting, *Nighthawks,* completed in 1942.

In Hopper's painting, the ordinary people at the counter are lost in their thoughts. No one is talking. They have stopped, each one, to have a cup of coffee or a bite to eat. The minutes tick by. Hopper seems to invite us to move on. At the same time, he seems to say, "Stay for awhile."

Snapshots of American Life

When Hopper first began painting, movies and automobiles were new inventions. Both had a big effect on his painting. When Hopper had trouble painting, he went to the movies. When times were bad, he went to the movies three or four times a week. He loved to sit in the dark and watch the movie. Sometimes Jo would go with him, but often he went alone. He looked at things the way a camera does. The pictures he painted from life were often like snapshots or scenes from a movie. Many of his pictures have the kind of lighting and point of view that we see in movies.

Get to Know Edward Hopper

In 1930, Edward and Jo Hopper bought land on Cape Cod. Hopper designed a simple cottage overlooking the bay. It had a big window to let in the light for painting. The house had a special bed built extra-big for Hopper's long legs. From then on, they spent many summers there. He loved the salty air of the Cape. The sea winds reminded Hopper of his early summers in Massachusetts and Maine. He would paint all summer long.

Hopper Hits It Big

Cape Cod Morning (1950, Smithsonian American Art Museum, Washington, DC). Hopper chose a joyful subject for this painting. As the woman looks out her window, welcoming a new day on Cape Cod, she seems free. She is looking out across the open field, beyond the trees' shadows.

Chapter 4

On the Road

Cars were new in the 1920s. Not a lot of people had them. Edward and Jo Hopper decided to buy a car. It had lots of room for their easels and canvases and paints and palettes. Now they could set off down the road and travel anywhere. Hopper often returned over and over to a place he was painting. He sat inside his car and sketched. Yet, Hopper's scenes seem fresh. They look as if someone had one quick, clear look from a car window while driving by.

Hopper and Jo spent a lot of time traveling, so roads and railroads fill Hopper's paintings. Yet, his scenes show stillness. Nothing is moving. Big, empty spaces in his paintings make us want to move on down the road. At the same time, they always offer an invitation to stay. The feelings in Hopper's paintings are feelings that Americans still have today. So, even though Hopper painted a long time ago, people are drawn to his paintings.

On the Road

South Truro Post Office (1930, Private Collection). The Hoppers' summer home was located in rural Truro, on Cape Cod.

Get to Know Edward Hopper

In his many paintings of Cape Cod, Hopper often focused on architecture. In *South Truro Post Office*, the color and shape of the buildings stand out against the landscape. Hopper especially liked the simplicity of old, wooden buildings like the ones shown in this painting.

Real-Life Subjects

Many people thought the things he painted were ugly. Hopper painted real life—things such as little alleys, freight cars, empty train stations. He painted people drinking coffee in a restaurant. He sketched deserted streets. Most artists did not choose to paint these kinds of everyday scenes. Perhaps they did not seem "artistic" enough. Hopper found them interesting, though. So did many other people. They liked his subjects and his special style. His paintings showed people how to see what he saw.

On the Road

The Hoppers made many summer trips. They drove across the western United States. Several times they went to Mexico. When they stopped the car, Jo and Hopper pulled out their art supplies. They sketched and painted. Jo also showed her paintings in exhibitions.

From 1941 to 1945, the United States was at war. Gasoline for the car was hard to get. So, in 1943, the Hoppers took a long train trip to get to Mexico. Later, in 1946, after the war, they were able to drive their car all the way down to Mexico. When they got there, they could not get gasoline for the car to come home! No one had told them that Mexico was still short of gas. Finally, they got some and came back. They were glad to get home, but they returned to Mexico several more times in the 1950s.

Get to Know Edward Hopper

Jo in Wyoming (1946, Private Collection). Hopper's wife Jo was his favorite model. In this watercolor painting, he shows her as she works during a trip to Wyoming.

Chapter 5

A Great American Artist

Edward Hopper worked for a long time before had any success. But his hard work paid off. He received many awards and honors in his lifetime. In 1933 the Museum of Modern Art in New York held a retrospective exhibition—a show that looked back over all Hopper's work. Hopper thought it would be the "kiss of death." He thought everyone would think he was finished painting. He was wrong. His success and fame continued to grow.

In 1945, Hopper was elected to the National Institute of Arts and Letters. He was one of four American artists featured at the Venice Biennale, a major international exhibition in 1955. The American Academy of Arts and Letters elected him as a member. In 1956–57, Hopper and Jo traveled to California where he was honored as artist-in-residence at the Huntington Hartford Foundation. Also in 1956, *Time* magazine put a

Hopper worked as an illustrator, a job he hated, while he tried to succeed as an artist. It was not until he was in his early forties that his hard work was rewarded and he became a famous artist.

A Great American Artist

photo of Hopper on its cover. The article was called "Silent Witness." In 1967, he was the featured artist in the United States Pavilion at the São Paulo Bienal in Brazil, another international exhibition.

The Last Years

During the 1950s and 1960s, Hopper was often ill and in the hospital. He painted as much as he could, but he completed fewer and fewer paintings. In the last years of his life, Hopper painted pictures that seemed to say good-bye. In *Sun in an Empty Room,* Hopper shows a room without furniture. It looks as if someone has just moved out. There are no people. There are no other objects. The sun streams in through the window, and the room is silent. His very last painting, done in 1965, is called *Two Comedians.*

On May 15, 1967, Edward Hopper died quietly in his studio in New York. He had lived in the same building for over fifty years. He was eighty-four years old. Less than a year later, Jo also died. She left most of Hopper's paintings, and many of her own, to the Whitney Museum of American Art in New York.

Celebrating the Artist

Since Hopper's death, museums in both the United States and Europe have celebrated his realistic scenes. Two large

Get to Know Edward Hopper

The House by the Railroad (1925, Museum of Modern Art, New York). It is said that Alfred Hitchcock based the setting for his 1960 horror thriller *Psycho* on this oil painting.

A Great American Artist

Chop Suey (1929, Private Collection). Hopper wanted to show real life and real people. Notice his use of lighting in the painting.

Get to Know Edward Hopper

retrospective exhibitions have been held in recent years. In 1995 the Whitney held an exhibition called "Edward Hopper and the American Imagination." The National Museum of Art, Smithsonian Institution, in Washington, DC, joined the Montgomery Museum of Fine Arts in Montgomery, Alabama, in a large retrospective in 1999–2000. It was called, "Edward Hopper, The Watercolors."

In her will, Hopper's wife, Jo, left all of his artwork to the Whitney Museum in New York. But you can still see many of his works on exhibit in museums all around the United States.

A Great American Artist

Second Story Sunlight (1960, Whitney Museum of American Art, New York). Edward Hopper's paintings have been in museums since the 1930s. Today, they are just as popular as they were then.

Timeline

1882—Edward Hopper is born on July 22 in Nyack, New York.

1889—Graduates from high school and enters art school.

1900—Begins study at the New York School of Art.

1903–04—Studies with Robert Henri.

1904—Begins teaching part-time at the New York School of Art.

1906–07—Makes his first trip to Paris.

1908—Moves to a studio in New York.

1909—Makes his second trip to Europe.

1910—Travels to Europe for the third and last time.

1913—Sells *Sailing* for $250. It is his first sale, and the last for ten years. Moves to Greenwich Village in New York.

1915–23—Works on etchings.

1923—Paints in Gloucester, Massachusetts, in the summer.

1924—Marries Josephine Nivison on July 9. They live in New York. They paint in Gloucester during the summer.

1925—Makes his first success with *House by the Railroad.*

1930—The Hoppers buy land at Cape Cod and begin building a summer house.

1933—First Hopper retrospective, at the Museum of Modern Art, New York.

1967—Edward Hopper dies, May 15, at his studio in New York.

1968—Jo Hopper dies March 6.

2007—Museum of Fine Arts in Boston holds exhibition of Hopper's greatest works.

2012—A major retrospective in Paris displays Hopper's works and his influences.

Glossary

canvas—Type of heavy cloth, stretched over a frame, that artists paint pictures on.

commercial art—Art that an artist is hired to do by a company, such as for ads.

etching—Drawing scratched onto a plate of metal, glass, or other material.

featured—Given special treatment; considered the main attraction.

ferryboat — Boat that takes people (and sometimes their cars) back and forth across a body of water.

harbor—Area of quiet waters where boats dock.

palette—Piece of wood or other surface for mixing the colors of oil paints—usually a handy size to hold.

retrospective—An exhibition that shows the work that an artist has done in the past.

vitality—Liveliness.

yacht—Boat used, not to earn a living, but just for the fun of boating.

Learn More

Books

Brooks, Susie. *Get Into Art: Telling Stories*. Boston: Kingfisher, 2015.

Burleigh, Robert. *Edward Hopper Paints His World*. New York: Henry Holt, 2015.

Ormison, Rosalind. *Edward Hopper Masterpieces*. London: Flame Tree, 2012.

Tuohy, Andy. *A to Z Great Modern Artists*. London: Octopus, 2015.

Websites

An Edward Hopper Scrapbook
americanart.si.edu/exhibitions/online/hopper/index.html

The Smithsonian's National Museum of American Art has put together a scrapbook about Edward Hopper's life and paintings. Take a tour through his life and art. Travel with the Hoppers on their journeys. Find out about his shows and paintings.

Artcyclopedia, The Fine Art Search Engine: Edward Hopper
www.artcyclopedia.com/artists/hopper_edward.html

This site has nearly 100 links to Hopper's paintings online, as well as books and articles about him and his work.

The Whitney Museum of American Art: Edward Hopper
collection.whitney.org/artist/621/EdwardHopper

The Whitney Museum's online collection includes links to Hopper's artwork as well as instructional audio tours.

Index

A
American Academy of Arts and Letters, 37
Armory Show, 14

C
Cape Cod, 30, 34
Chase, William Merritt, 8
city paintings, 25, 27, 29
commercial art, 12

D
death, 39

E
etchings, 14–16, 18
Europe, 8–10

G
Gloucester, Massachusetts, 18, 20

H
Henri, Robert, 8, 18
Hopper, Elizabeth (mother), 5–6
Hopper, Garret Henry (father), 5
Hopper, Marion (sister), 5

M
Mexico, 35
Museum of Modern Art, 37

N
New England paintings, 22, 25
New York City, NY 8, 10, 12, 14, 18, 20, 37, 39, 42
New York School of Art, 8, 18
Nivison, Josephine, 18, 20–22, 25, 29–30, 32, 35, 37, 39, 42
Nyack, New York, 5–6

O
oil painting, 16, 18, 24–25

P
Paris, France, 10

R
real-life paintings, 25, 34
Rehn, Frank, 18–20

S
success, 24

T
Time magazine, 37–39
traveling and painting, 32, 34–35

W
Washington Square, 14, 20
watercolors, 18–20, 25, 42
Whitney Museum of American Art, 39, 42

RECEIVED MAY 2 2016